ABUSE THIS WORD...

by PATRICK COSGROVE & LAWRENCE HUSSAR

ABUSE THIS WORD . . . is an original publication of Avon Books.
This work has never before appeared in book form.

AVON BOOKS
A division of
The Hearst Corporation
959 Eighth Avenue
New York, New York 10019

First Avon Printing, September, 1980

Printed in the U.S.A.

To Karen Jo, Ron and our parents

Here's how to
operate this book:

Abuse the word
"paradox" in a sentence.

These are examples:

The scholar discovered a paradox.	There are a paradox at the lake.	I met a paradox.

Not funny.	Semi-funny.	Very funny.

Okay?
Now abuse the word
officiate in a sentence.

Efram grew sick from officiate.

Abuse the word hierarchy.

The higher we sing, the hierarchy.

meteor

"Aren't you going to introduce meteor aunt?"

meringue

Meringue tang died.

1.

2.

oscillate

Oscillate I missed my train.

gargoyle

Betty found work in Bayonne as a cigargoyle.

saxophone

During saxophone call is very annoying.

grandiose

He'll be sorry if he doesn't pay back the grandiose.

adequate

Adequate years ago if I had a better offer.

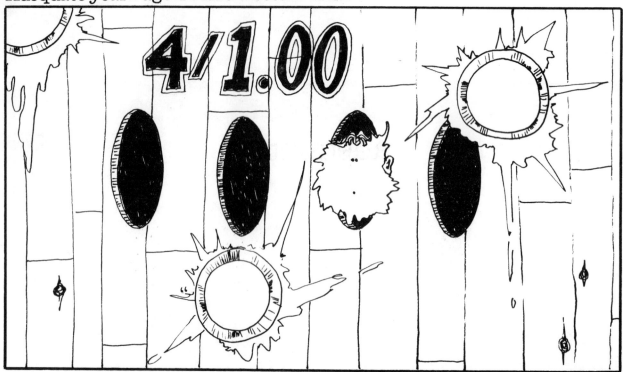

paroxysm

Cleaning up after a paroxysm mess.

scallops

Scallops stairs I'd like to fondle.

filibuster

During rush hour it's necessary to filibuster capacity.

somersault

Some of these are onion. Somersault.

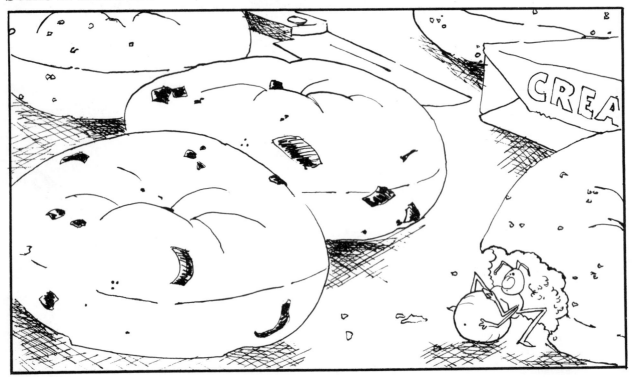

liverwurst

Beatrice was resigned to liverwurst years with Cecil.

rutabaga

Oswald was rutabaga fart and then open it in Essie's face.

mutineer

The reactor attendant developed a mutineer.

acetone

Acetone it will be 6:51 and ten seconds...
Acetone it will be 6:51 and twenty seconds...

fluorescent

If you're looking for men's wear,
this fluorescent the one you want.

vitamin

Vitamin fall in love?

Czechoslovakia

Vakia's been bugging me for the rent;
this czechoslovakia down for awhile.

Naugahyde®

"Can I come out now?" "Naugahyde.®"

nitrogen

During the day tro' scotch, but at nitrogen.

50

protocol

For the best lesson you must know the right protocol.

dishonesty

Dishonesty nearest star.

gingham

The Catskill comic kept zing gingham.

asterisk

Asterisk you take when you don't have insurance.

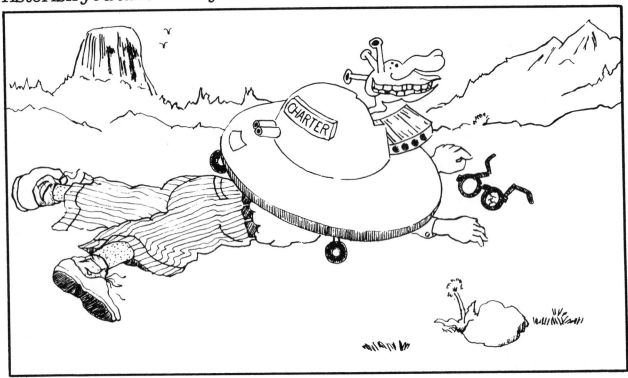

fortuitous

Fortuitous a very generous meal.

asphalt

We could've won until the asphalted his serve.

acoustic

One plays pool with acoustic.

UNACCEPTABLE

ACCEPTABLE

commentator

The Idaho is a commentator.

bizarre

Ivan got to bizarre of all Russia.

cultivate

The small religious sect was a cultivate.

dromedary

"Would ya'll dromedary cow?"

speculate

"If you're all tied up, should I speculate for dinner?"

honorary

The cruel boys commented honorary face.

kumquat

"Ya'll kumquat or the kids'll hear ya."

cadaver

She was all the girl he cadaver want.

gamma-rays

Watch Gamma-rays Gampa after they drink prune juice.

carnivorous

A used carnivorous guaranteed.

complain

Some come peanut. Some complain.

formaldehyde

"Formaldehyding places came de Indians mit bows 'n arrows!"

litany

"Litany good farts lately?"

boisterous

Boisterous differently than girls.

catatonic

"Better give that catatonic – he looks like he could use one."

Schenectady

The leg bone's schenectady thigh bone.

urinal

Urinal lot of trouble if Dr. Pomerance finds you.

horrify

"Would I be a horrify took your gift?"

tapestry

"If you tapestry you're s'posed to get three wishes."

grocery

He's either grocery's stupid.

clemency

"Let's call up Clemency what he says."

argyle

"Argyle beat your guy any day."

horizon

He couldn't draw horizon the right place.

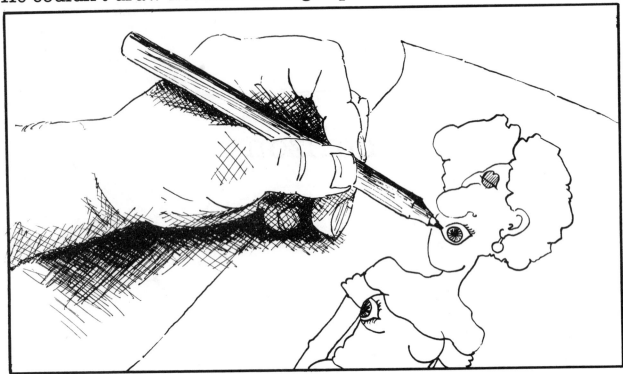

artifacts

"These artifacts of life."

porcelain

You'll stay porcelain that merchandise.

corduroy

"Here's the corduroy owe you."

bifocal

Bifocal get into bed with anyone.

Deuteronomy

"The film society is deuteronomy with a special award."

gourmet

"I'm afraid the gourmet scare you."

phenomenal

The proprietor charged Ralph phenomenal leg.

literature

Literature feet might make you trip.

Bavaria

This book is bavarias authors.